Gastón Fernández

Apparent Breviary

translated from Spanish by KM Cascia

 WORLD POETRY

Apparent Breviary by Gastón Fernández
Copyright © Mariana Fernández, 2025
Introduction and English translation copyright © KM Cascia, 2025

Originally published as *Breviario aparente* (Lima: tRpode, 2006)

First Edition, First Printing, 2025
ISBN 978-1-954218-34-5

World Poetry Books
New York, NY
worldpoetrybooks.com

Available to the trade through Asterism Books
Distributed in the UK and Europe by Turnaround Publisher Services
Subscriptions and standing orders available directly from the publisher

Library of Congress Control Number: 2025930685

Cover design by Andrew Bourne
Typesetting by Don't Look Now
Printed in Lithuania by BALTO Print

World Poetry Books is a 501(c)(3) nonprofit and charitable organization founded in 2017 in New York City, affiliated with the Humanities Institute and the Translation Program at the University of Connecticut (Storrs), and a member of the Community of Literary Magazines and Presses (CLMP).

World Poetry's publications and programs are made possible with funding from the Poetry Foundation and the New York State Council on the Arts, as well as generous support from individual donors and subscribers.

Introduction: Gastón the Ghost

The Apparent Professor

Gastón Fernández Carrera was born January 28, 1940, to a reasonably comfortable family, in Lima, Peru. He went to private Catholic schools, then studied law in Peru from 1957 until 1963. In 1969, he left to attend graduate school in Belgium, where he lived for the rest of his life. He worked as a museum guide while studying for a doctorate in Art History, which he earned from the University of Louvain in 1973. He taught art history, mostly in Brussels, for the rest of his career. He was the author of four books on aesthetics and one travelogue, all written in French. He died on January 20, 1997, just short of his fifty-seventh birthday.

That's the tidy story of a tidy, if somewhat abbreviated, life. Apparently the way he wanted it told. And true, in its way. It simply leaves a great deal out. Especially the fact that Gastón was, in his native Spanish, a literary writer of skill and ambition, with extraordinary control. This was true before he left Peru in the late '60s. He continued to pursue his writing in Europe, alongside his studies and academic work, throughout the '70s. By the mid-'80s, he was publishing often, in some important journals. But toward the end of the decade, for reasons unknown, Gastón changed course. He turned his attention from stories and poems to theory and criticism. And he began writing in French full-time, mostly reserving Spanish for personal letters. His complete literary work in his native language consisted of two manuscripts, both published only after his death, though completed a full decade earlier.

Gastón who?

Gastón's biography moves the same way his writing does: a coincidence perhaps, but it feels deliberate. The basic facts, once assembled, convey little. A haze accumulates. And hangs. Only later, in retrospect, what was and was not significant becomes clear and the real narrative emerges.

In 1975, not long after he finished his doctorate, he published his first literary work. He had one more small publication in 1978. Then came the peak of his literary activity: five pieces in important Peruvian journals between 1981 and 1987. It wasn't lack of material that slowed his output; Gastón wrote continuously, producing more than 500 pages of fiction in his lifetime. Rather, it was a question of temperament.

Gastón was formally and stylistically ambitious in his writing, but less so in forging a career. He most likely pursued an academic path as a way of avoiding all that. He mailed his fiction to friends. Once a piece had made the rounds, he would file it away with the rest. This is how most of his work was read in his own lifetime. That anyone outside his immediate circle got to see any of it, ever, is largely down to those friends themselves.

His best friend, from the late '70s until his death, was the novelist and feminist literary scholar Helena Araújo. Originally from Colombia, she lived and worked in Switzerland. The two of them wrote to and visited one another constantly, and their published letters reveal a deep connection rooted in a shared love of art and literature.

Another close friend was the Cuban poet José Kozer. Based in New York, he was one of the leading figures in the neo-baroque school of poetry that was then in flower. As with Araújo, the published letters between Gastón and Kozer reflect an uncommonly deep friendship. These two influential friends might have been the key to Gastón's brief surge of publications. Their letters are full of chatter about it.

Another important friend was the Peruvian poet Enriqueta Belevan. They first met in the early '60s. While Gastón was busy in Europe, Belevan published a book in 1978 and another in 1984. Gastón read a review of her second book in a Peruvian magazine that reached him in Brussels, and he asked his mother to get Enriqueta's address for him. They maintained a warm, rambling correspondence for years.

While Gastón had other correspondents, Araújo, Kozer, and Belevan became crucial to his literary legacy since they knew Gastón was much more than the apparent professor. All three would have known that, past a certain point (around 1988), he wasn't really writing in Spanish anymore, though there is not much in the published letters about his turn toward French. In their letters, they simply go on talking about art and philosophy, their vacations and illnesses.

When Gastón died, that was where things stood. A writer's writer, best known for being unknown, who had published just a few extraordinary things, a long time ago. Well-respected by those who had known him, but more often heard about than read. Maybe just a little bit of a cult figure in Lima. But not really. Not yet.

Gastón the Great

Gastón's literary work in Spanish, as mentioned, consisted of two completed manuscripts. One was a collection of stories. Titled *Relatos aparentes* ("Apparent Stories"), it consisted of 33 prose pieces, all of them titled *relato aparente* and numbered i–xxxiii. The other was a group of 100 single-page poems called *Brevario aparente* ("Apparent Breviary"). Both manuscripts were eventually published in Peru, in excellent editions. The stories came out in 2002, edited by José Ignacio Padilla. The poems, edited by my friend Renato Gómez, were published in 2006.

So, ten years after he died, Gastón's literary achievements in his native language were finally recognized. Two books, 33 stories, 100 poems, linked thematically, sharing a distinctive, mature style. All written by an unknown professor, living in exile, who had since died in obscurity.

This is perilously close to the plot of certain Borges stories. And perfectly legible as a neo-baroque backstory, a character sketch that *neobarroquistas* like Néstor Perlongher or one of the Lamborghini brothers might casually toss in as an aside. It was compelling to Padilla, Gómez, and their peers, and their editions did make Gastón into something of a cult figure, at least in Lima. When Renato gave me both books, in New York in 2009, I, too, was an instant convert.

Gáston's posthumous readership grew quite a bit further when the Peruvian-born and Buenos Aires–based neo-baroque poet Reynaldo Jiménez devoted two issues of his journal to a vast dossier on Gastón: nearly 500 pages of stories, poems, and correspondence, a selection of Gastón's writing on art, as well as critical essays by Padilla, Gómez, Américo Ferrari, Octavio Armand, and Jiménez himself.

Taken together, these three publications were enough to cement Gastón's reputation, at least in Latin America. He was a major writer, one of the best of his period—the '70s and '80s.

There remains the question of whether Gastón can fairly be considered a neo-baroque writer. Gastón himself would certainly have artfully dodged and avoided the question while rejecting the label, along with any associated aesthetic practices or opinions. Which is exactly what a *neobarroquista* would do. The leading figures of the neo-baroque movement describe it as "a certain operation of the folding of form and content" (Perlongher), a process of "obliterating the signifier of a given signified, but not replacing it with another, but rather by a chain of signifiers which progress metonymically and which end by circumscribing the absent signified, tracing an orbit around it" (Severo Sarduy). That "chain of signifiers" is a hell of a good way to describe Gastón's prose, while his poetry is made almost entirely out of "the absent signified."

Gastón the Poet

Enriqueta Belevan recalls that very soon after the beginning of her correspondence with Gastón,

> ...there began to arrive, in manila envelopes, 10 office-sized pages with a poem numbered out of order: 4? 8? 10? 15? 18. Like that. They arrived with discipline, every 10 days, 10 pages. Everyone in my house participated in this. From the extremely surprised postman to my own super-amused mother. The few friends who came over to practice playing the recorder saw the envelopes, more and more of them all the time, and laughed nervously. Ten envelopes later I gathered together all the pages and had the Apparent Breviary *complete before my eyes.*

That would have been in 1984, but the poems were written in 1980–81. (There was only the one manuscript, typewritten.) Gastón finished it, held onto it for a few years, then mailed it to Belevan. It is unclear whether he showed it to or talked about it with anyone else. Belevan did, allowing it to be photocopied and eventually scanned. She also loaned the manuscript itself out, once, to a friend who kept it for several months, wrote a poem about it called "The Antenna's Perfection Is the Error It Transmits" and refused to discuss it further, ever again.

In an essay on Gastón's poems called "Aspects of Failure," Renato Gómez says that his "sole and authentic intention" in publishing "the Breviary" as a book was "to prove that the power of the original would be annulled by publication." In fact, throughout the process, he sensed the manuscript was resisting his efforts to make it into a book. Technical problems, legibility issues, uncertain readings, burnout, all delayed the process. "This gathering of feelings," he says, "was exerting itself to not become a thing." But he did it anyway. And in the end, Renato realized, "There is no manuscript of the *Breviary*, the true *Breviary* is only the manuscript, one manuscript."

I may disagree to some extent, but I certainly understand the phenomenon—common to everyone who approached these poems over the years—of getting a little too wrapped up in them and kind of losing your head. There's simply so much white space to fall into. You start to consider things. You wonder if the poems may, in fact, actually be the white space, with the words there just to shape it. To draw attention to that "absent signified" mentioned above. Which is the (apparent?) absence of God, an absence gestured at in the overtly religious language, yes, but also in the rest of the vocabulary, in the echo of the Psalms contained in the form. And in the titular concept, a breviary: a book containing everything required to pray the Liturgy of the Hours, the seven-times-daily prayer cycle of monastic tradition. The poems seem as fragmented as a Dead Sea scroll, as incomplete as half an antiphony, as quiet as a sermon heard from the way-back of an echoey church. They shove a word like "Lord" in your face and leave you no option but to notice your own response.

And something emerges from the words, or from the space between the letters. Or maybe it emerges with the words. Maybe you emerge where the words are. Anyway, you encounter. And you don't notice that you're not wondering how fast you should be reading, or even that you're turning pages. You're being pulled through, toward something, without focusing overmuch on the process, as with a rosary or some other patterned prayer. The poems provide the pattern, the rhythm. And if they can provide that, they can perhaps provide other, more theologically complex encounters with the absent signified they circumscribe.

Gastón in English

Unexpected encounters with Divine silence are not exactly what I read poetry for. Or at least that was not the case in 2009, when Renato Gómez gave me Gastón's books. I got my head around the prose fairly easily. But the *Breviary* made me squirm. I was so uncomfortable I didn't even want to ask myself why. I read it once or twice and didn't pick it up again for three years. But I kept it with me.

When I went back to it, in 2012, it was fall in Chicago. I was living in a flophouse hotel, working in a restaurant where they had me slicing bucket after bucket of pig ears all day long. Things were bad, and there was every reason to suppose they would get worse. So, I quit showing up to the pig ear slicing job, translated the *Breviary* over the course of a couple of weeks, and when the rent came due again, I left town. I don't think I even re-read it before beginning. Just took it to a coffee shop and started in. It still made me squirm, so I just squirmed my way through it. That draft got revised over the winter and filed away, only to be pulled out and pondered over the years. It was then substantially revised, almost re-translated, for this edition.

Still makes me squirm. Calls to mind a Lew Welch poem I read often in Chicago, where he says the sky in the Midwest makes you "understand why the Bible is the way it is." The *Breviary* seems that way to me too, like it suggests something both awesome and unknowable. Especially now.

The technical issues largely stemmed from the sparseness of the language, and how much of it is repeated from one poem to the next. It needs as few words as possible, so there was a fair bit of agonizing. How to render infinitives, for example, or which prepositions were absolutely necessary, and which were not. To keep or discard the definite article. And along with that, the need to preserve the repetition of certain key words, which meant rendering them in the best way for multiple points in the text.

The biggest single change, reflecting a much deeper familiarity with the Bible (in both languages) than I had years ago, was pushing the vocabulary toward choices that emphasized the allusions and echoes in the original. Often, I had squirmed my way to the wrong decision, or just didn't quite hear what was there. That needed correcting, though it was important not to make these allusions more forceful than they are in the Spanish.

It is difficult, as a translator, to feel all too confident in anything beyond having done the work in a case like this. For one thing, if my friend Renato is right, and there is only the one Breviary—the poetry of which was lost when it was published as a book—then this translation is *a priori* absolutely doomed. At least in any normal understanding of translation. If the original text is a copy of a copy, devoid of poetry, then there can be no poetry in the target language except what the translator makes.

This is not exactly my position; just something I tried to keep in mind. I did a careful rendering here, and something of *Brevario aparente* has survived the transformation into *Apparent Breviary*. But virtually every translation choice meant accepting the loss of something that felt a shame to lose. This edition could easily be littered with footnotes offering alternate readings of a given word or line. Constructing the best version of the Breviary in translation, the one I have in my head—where all the white space becomes three dimensional, and the poems branch out as different planes connected by a given word or concept filling all that space—would require technology from a better future than the one we're living in.

But as I worked on this through the fall and into winter, as bombs fell on Gaza like water, an untranslatable poem about the silence of God came to seem proper for the future we do inhabit. And the work grew heavier as my encounter with the reality the poems describe became more and more urgent. One beholds horrors, and one weeps, then returns to work. The silence remains.

This translation is dedicated to Khaled Nabhan.

—*KM Cascia*

Works Cited

Fernández, Gastón.
   Relatos aparentes. Lima: Ediciones del signo lotófago, 2002.
   Brevario aparente. Lima: tRpode, 2006.
   El ignaro triunfo de la razón. Sao Paolo: Lumme Editora, 2013.

Perlongher, Néstor. *Caribe transplatino.* Sao Paolo: Iluminuras, 1991.

Brevario aparente

Apparent Breviary

1

Dividir las venas

veo que es menos accesible que la
profundidad
           del aire

desde mi sitio

he visto
que el aire en efecto no tiene

velocidad.

El aire entonces,
Señor

1

Divide the veins

I see is less accessible than
depth
              of air

from my place

I've seen
that indeed air has no

velocity.

Then air,
Lord.

2

Cada vez que veo el sol creo en un género
opuesto. Necesariamente
la verdadera ausencia   esa extremada
libertad
               mis manos, replican: la sangre no asesina.

Es el mismo tigre sin embargo
que tiembla   otra vez

en mis manos

2

Every time I see the sun I believe in
an opposite. Necessarily
the true absence   that extreme
liberty
            my hands, they reply: blood doesn't kill.

It remains the same tiger,
who trembles   again

in my hands

3

Por qué.

       Por qué.

¿No hay algo en el mito interior?
Recuerdo la continencia que no hay en la
sangre,
ese mito extranjero. El hombre me exhala
el poderío del ave, el ave
no exhala
el poderío
del ave.

Sangre
Señor

3

Why.

                    Why.

Is there nothing in the inner myth?
I remember the moderation that is not in
blood,
that foreign myth. Man breathes me
the power of birds, birds
do not breathe
the power
of birds.

Blood
Lord

4

Por qué entonces una serenidad en los
arbustos   en los gatos
de cada día
mediodía   la noche que se advierte
como metete   como lastre
los objetos que se quedan   es verdad

                        perfectos

(yo busco esa medida en que el agua
no se quede
para siempre. Esa medida del agua

esa medida en que el agua

              se vierta

sin canto
general   sin prosa

Sin poema

Poemario, Señor

4

Why then a serenity in the
bushes   in the cats
every day
midday   the night that warns
it meddles   its ballast
objects that remain   it's true

                                  perfect

(I seek that measure where water
does not remain
forever. That measure of water

that measure where water

                pours

with no general
song   no prose

With no poem

Poems, Lord

5

Tengo razón
Quizás otra vez
              mirando

sepa   el verdadero repique está
en los labios.   Lo extraño
                      Lo muerto
                      Lo mirado

Y mirar no es posible.
Y todas las cosas que he hecho ayer han sido

bien.

La prueba

el sol

5

I am right
Perhaps again
                looking

I know   the true peal is
on the lips.   The strange
                      The dead
                      The seen

And to look is not possible.
And all the things I've done in the past have been

good.

The proof

the sun

6

El mal es un
menor

el agua resiste   es dura

como el agua   todo

se mimetiza

           Mi rostro es vecino   el cafre
           es vecino
           el inmigrante   es   recuerdo

           y un grano es factible

           la mierda es
           importante.

La efigie se tuerce y
es efigie.

Tiempo   reflejo en la imagen.   Tiempo creencia
de imagen.   Peldaños.

Siempre
las balas dibujan   creyendo
escalinatas
de oro

6

Evil is something
minor

water resists   hard

as water   mimics

everything

        Neighbor is my face   the savage
        is neighbor
        the immigrant   is   memory

        and grain is feasible

        shit is
        important.

The effigy twists and
is an effigy.

Time   reflect on the image.   Time belief
in image.   Stairs.

Always
the bullets   believing   sketch
staircases
of gold

7

Se ha dicho: miro de preferencia
en las pantallas   allá donde se
mira de ordinario el centro, la
totalidad

yo
   las esquinas.   Los muertos   donde

tiene lugar
la maravilla

7

It was said: I prefer to watch
screens   where you
ordinarily watch the center, the
totality

I
    the corners.   Dead places   where

wonders
happen

8

Erudito del vientre

Erudito del peso.　　　Del soplo.

Erudito del labio.

Qué

　en el acto.　　　En el singular
　　　　　　　　En lo propio.

Un siniestro, una memoria
ya.

(Erudito del agua, del silo,

erudito del agua
las veces que he puesto un adjetivo sobre el
nombre el hombre no ha tenido
cara

8

Scholar of womb

Scholar of weight.　　　Of breath.

Scholar of lips.

What

   in the act.　　　In the singular
　　　　　　　　　　　In the personal.

Someone wicked, now a
memory.

(Scholar of water, of silo,

scholar of water
when I've put an adjective over the
name the man has had no
face

9

Cambiarse, del estómago a la luz

Asegurar que la luz se acuerpa
en mi sombra
un segundo

(Tanta prosecución

                    latente
                    visible
                    momentánea

realidad
sin pérdidas)

Hacer   —fingir creer   que   suda el miembro
                                            ruge el miembro
                                            gana el miembro

el velo

9

Transform, from stomach to light

Ensure   that light embodies
self in my shadow
a second

(So much pursuit

                      latent
                      visible
                      momentary

reality
without loss)

Make   —feign belief   that   the member sweats
                                                      the member roars
                                                      the member wins

the veil

10

Ayer supuse
                          otra vez   para poder
hablar

que voltearía la cabeza   —

(la mano pierde el sentido
dejada demasiado tiempo
en el seno

y poco tiempo es deseo

En el medio   queda
el azar,
ruidos como de casualidad
rehechos.   Al voltear

la muerte
                de pie
no tiembla,
no se mueve)

10

Yesterday I supposed
                       once again   you would
turn

your head so we could talk   —

(the hand loses feeling
left for too long
on the breast

and desire is a short time

In the center   chance
remains,
noises by chance
remade.   Turn around

death
                 stands there
does not tremble,
does not move)

11

No soy yo
el mudo

la realidad se vierte, ella,
en el revés de ojos
en la espalda del labio

El viento.

El libro.   Vertientes de ojo

Señor,
por qué sino   el sin embargo
si la esperanza se vierte en edificios   si
las manos agarran
recipientes

aire

astro de pie preguntando si la
claridad   es

realmente

11

I'm not the
mute one

reality spills, her,
on reversed eyes
on the lip's back

The wind.

The book.   Spilling eyes.

Lord,
why if not   the nonetheless
if hope spills over buildings   if
hands grasp
contain

air

footnote asking if
clarity   is

really

12

El ave　　　es

fuego,

venas

ojos, hueco hacia
arriba

siendo:　　　la vida precipita un flujo inerte
en el peso　　y alma es aire

                                                    un libro
                                                    un rastro
                                                    no soy yo

                                                    el habla

12

The bird   is

fire,

veins

eyes, hollow heading
upward

being: life precipitates an inert flow
in weight   and soul is air

                        a book
                        a trace
                        I am not

                        speech

13

Ponte ahí

Quisiera entrar en la frente

La cima de los templos es corta
La cúspide de los cabellos   es corta

y si hablo
pierdo.

Y si hablo
en los cuerpos —

¡Esa tiniebla
esa casa
las aves cuando miran!

13

Right over there

I'd rather go forehead first

The temple mount is short
The hair's peak   is short

and if I speak
I lose.

And if I talk
about the bodies—

That darkness
that house
the way the birds gaze!

14

La furia es un nombre

O saber a un poeta en un libro.　　O poner
la conciencia en
la nube.　　Colocar
a un patriarca　　en los labios,
limpiarme una revolución en los
labios

(Asesinar al hombre, organizar
el cuerpo a fin de comprender
　　　　　　　　　　　el frío

el arma

dar muerte al fonema para que no haya
muerte　　y
asesinar al hombre
sin razón
sin prosa
sin poema

14

Rage is a noun

Either know a poet in a book   Or put
one's conscience on
a cloud.   Place a
patriarch   on one's lips,
wipe a revolution from my
lips

(To murder man, to organize
the body with the goal of understanding
                                  the cold

the weapon

death to the phoneme so there will be no
death   and
murder man
no reason
no prose
no poem

15

Que sea el escarnio

Que se lea

Pasar de una revista al rostro,
de una página a la exacta   vindicta
universal, porque el escarnio
gravita en la boca
entre los poros de
letras   viaja en
los dedos

promoviendo   proponiendo figurarme
entre las piedras

incorporándome para recomenzar
el ave   el sexo

el tiempo

15

Let there be derision

Let it be read

Pass from magazine to face,
from page to precise   universal
vengeance, because derision
centers in the mouth
between pores of
letters   travels on
fingers

promoting   proposing to figure myself
among the stones

incorporate myself to begin again
birds   sex

time

16

Ver el mundo instantáneo
cuando no hay
objeto.

Caer en los registros del sol.

Rememorar sin que la necesidad de alterar la huella del
 miembro
se refleje
en la cara

Hablar y que la fascinación
se calle.

16

See the world   instantaneous
when there is no
object

Fall in registers of sun.

Remember without need to alter the traces
reflected
in the face

Speak and let fascination
fall silent.

17

Yo era como antes   y no
se tendrá vergüenza

todos
preguntan si queda el
cauce mismo   si tiembla
la idea del vuelo,
la certidumbre   extranjera
de lo vivo   la necesidad
del lecho   de la danza
                        en la frente.

Escarnio en la frente
en la medalla

en la sangre

Señor,
si en las medidas del ojo
el aire se enfrenta con las certidumbres
del vano

si la página
no cae   de escarnio

de tranquilidad

17

I was as before   and will
not be ashamed

everyone
asks if the same
riverbed remains   if there trembles
the idea of flight,
the strange   certainty
of the living   the necessity
of bed   of dance
                    on the brow.

Derision on the brow
on the medal

in the blood

Lord,
if in the eye's measure
air confronts the certainties
of vanity

if the page
does not fall   from derision

from tranquility

18

Si digo: sobrevivir
en el hombre

Por qué   qué inclemencia en el   vértigo
de contornear
al hombre

en la sien.

Y en los labios la memoria
se tuerce,
no se pierde.

En balas, en los libros, el hálito   sólo
ya es sombra

conducto.   El fuego   sólo

ya es infancia

18

If I say: survive
in man

Why   what severity in the   vertigo
of tracing
man

on the temple.

And on lips memory
twists,
not lost.

In bullets, in books, breath   is now
only shadow

conduct.   Fire   is now

only childhood

19

Pasar de la página volteada
a la deposición
                      exacta
de la mirada,
sin apelarse,
sin llaga

Y voltear la cara es un
símbolo,

patrocinarse

minuto tras minuto en el otro   en dos o tres miembros
sin que el cuerpo lo sepa, ponerse
sin prisa, sin problemas
entre la mirada y la
muerte

Leer que el símbolo sea

y el libro
y el hambre

escarnio en el fuego

19

To pass from turned page
to the exact
                    deposition
of the gaze,
without appeal,
without wounds

And the turn of one's face is a
symbol,

to represent one's self

minute after minute in the other   in two or three parts
without the body knowing, place one's self
unhurriedly, with no problem
between the gaze and
death

Read what the symbol may be

and the book
and the hunger

derision in fire

20

Otro   hacia
el vano.   En el deseo del otro hay la idea,
donde el silencio sin duda no es peor
que el tacto. En el vientre del otro:

un esquema,

la espontaneidad de un ruido

un afiche   un cuerpo.

un ruido

20

Other   toward
vanity.   In the other's desire is the idea,
where silence doubtless is no worse
than touch. In the other's belly:

a diagram,

the spontaneity of a noise

a poster   a body.

a noise

21

Hablar y
el frío

casi iba a decir: nieva

Adelante ha continuado
la mirada   o me he
detenido.

Hombres en los miembros   o
en la mujer   el otro
atrás, en
términos.

21

To speak   and
the cold

I almost said: it's snowing

The gaze has gone on
ahead   or I have
stopped.

Men in the members   or
in woman   the other
behind, at
the end.

22

De casualidad   amatorio

ir a la casa del
vulgar.   Vomitar con él

en su lengua   en su frente

asumir de amor   en su lema

en mi facies
en un haz

el sol
el agua

22

By amorous   chance

go to the home of
the vulgar.   Vomit with him

on the tongue   on the brow

take on love   in the slogan

in my features
in a sheaf

sun
water

23

Al sitio del vietnamita.

A su palpitación.   a la
imposibilidad.

a su luz, plegaria muerta   en
su cara.   balbucear relicarios

pretéritos
pluscuamperfectos   puros

y poner la lengua en su sueño
para ver.

No decir:
nosotros

23

To the Vietnamese girl's place.

To her palpitation.   to the
impossibility.

to her light, dead prayers   in
her face.   babbling reliquaries

preterite
pluperfect   pure

and place tongue in her dream
to see.

Not to say:
us

24

Un ave. Un movimiento.

El vuelo y el canto   es

el mundo.

Singular.

                    Punto.

Vano:

No existen   allí
el movimiento y
el canto   no hay vuelo
ni inmovilidad.   Veo mi sitio ocupado
por un infante

la capacidad del punto
                    de fundar
la impotencia.

24

A bird.   A motion.

Flight and song   is

the world.

Singular.

                        Point.

Vanity:

There   movement
and song do
not exist   there is neither flight
nor stillness.   I see my place taken
by an infant

the period's capacity
                        to establish
impotence.

25

No decir:
nosotros.　　No decir silencio
　　　　　　No decir maravillas.

Cerrar las líneas de la luz en el cuello
del hombre,
promover el vano
en la sombra　para comenzar.

El inicio.　　El verbo.

Voltear el cuello y que el vientre no intuya la epifanía
del hombre

que el número
sea.

Que el hombre se mire　fuego en las manos

fuego
en el vano

25

Not to say:
us.   Not to say silence.
            Not to say wonders.

Close the lines of light on the neck
of man,
promote vanity
in shadow   so to begin.

The beginning.   The word.

Twist neck and belly does not guess the epiphany
of the man

the number
may be.

May man behold himself   fire in his hands

fire
in vanity

26

El deseo no pertenece.

Los pechos se llevan
como el labio

no preguntan
la circularidad   o la imperfección

si el deseo
les es.

Maravilla.

Siniestro

                    Voz

permanencia
en el aire

26

Desire is no one's.

Breasts worn
like a lip

don't ask
circularity   or imperfection

if desire
is theirs.

Miracle.

Wicked

        Voice

sojourn
in air

27

El deseo no pertenece

el labio se lleva como
memoria

ojos

muerte adelante

sin volición
sin dilema

sin aire

27

Desire is no one's

lip worn like
memory

eyes

death   ahead

without will
without dilemma

without air

28

Escribir

para hablar

Transformar el gozo del encuentro en encuentro el deseo

en anterioridad.

Reunir se.

borrar

28

Write

    to   speak

Transform the pleasure
of the encounter in
the encountering   desire

in the prior.

To gath   er.

to erase

29

Porque no es que nieve.

Generaciones de rayos
de emblemas de
sangre

que no hay.

Leer
la sangre en
otro

caminar otra
vez.

Encontrar al otro
en el vano mismo

en mis uñas. Sitio pequeño
entre su realidad y mi sombra

Ábside.

Vitrina.

Velocidad.

Interior.

29

Because it's not snowing.

Generations of lightning
of emblems   of
blood

there is not.

Read
the blood in
another

walk   once
more.

Encounter the other
in vanity itself

in my fingernails.   Small place
between their reality and my shadow

Apse.

Glass.

Velocity.

Interior.

30

El deseo no pertenece

y muerde como el encuentro

al sitio

perfecta articulación

Sin desmesura.

Nada.

Horda.

Vitrina

Habla.

30

Desire is no one's

and bites like the encounter

does the place

perfect   articulation

                                     Without excess.

                                     Nothing.

Horde.

Glass

Speech

31

La inocencia.

por ejemplo.   Sonoridad

verosímil, igual
que sangre.

Ojo en la nuca, labio
en el agua

aire   en
el arma,

muerte

del sol a nieve.

31

Innocence.

for example.　　　Plausible

sonority, same
as blood.

Nape eye behind, lip
in water

air　　in
the weapon,

death

from sun to snow.

32

El deseo no acompaña

se queda

como ronda.

El miembro   que falta
en la silla

es deseo,

entreverado en el
                    aire

en la lengua

32

Desire does not accompany

it remains

like a round.

The member   lacking in
the chair

is desire,

interspersed in
                air

on the tongue

33

Cuál es la libertad
del gesto

creer rozar

el inicio
del aire

Crear
rozar
el espacio de un ojo

término   que es
no el espacio del
tigre

no las manos

33

What is liberty
of gesture

to believe to touch

air's
beginning

To create
to touch
the space of an eye

term   which is
no tiger's
space

no hands

34

Al sitio del argentino
del camboyano

del rostro

al de la
precisión
infinitesimal   de la

muerte.

Al alma.

Aire
Señor

si la precisión
es el alma

si muerte es
el alma   para que
mi posibilidad   se
ponga

34

To the Argentine's place
the Cambodian's

the face's

to the place of
the infinitesimal
precision   of

death.

To the soul.

Air
Lord

if precision
is the soul

if death is
the soul   for which
my possibility   places

35

Es la figura   el signo
de la ilusión

en el libro,
en un caballo.

En la mesa
inacabada.   En sus   codos.

El gesto solo   anuncia   ya
sitio,
el estertor
          fuego

sangre
siguiente

35

The figure is   the sign
of illusion

in the book,
on a horse.

On the unfinished
table.   In their   elbows.

The sole gesture   now   announces
place,
death rattle
          fire

blood
following

36

Al sitio del hombre
en un
         ojo.

Al sitio
del miedo.

Se dificulta el pasaje
hacia la
         muerte
en el otro.   Se esquema.

En un libro.
En la paloma

en el recuerdo

del habla

36

To a man's place
in an
         eye.

To the place
of fear.

The voyage grows difficult
toward
                  death
in the other.   Schemes.

In a book.
In a dove

in the memory

of speech

37

Se dificulta en el día

A la luz de una vela   el
hombre presta su
serenidad
              al fuego.

Adjetivo.

El día   fausto
              en que morirán
              los olmos.

Sangre

Señor

37

Grows difficult on the day.

In the light of a candle   the
man lends his
serenity
              to fire.

Adjective.

The auspicious   day
                  when all elms
                  shall die.

Blood

Lord

38

En los cuellos,

en páginas.

Cuellos crecientes
                        vientres
en los que sé

libros,
caleidoscopios

sexos

recogidos

entre vidrios

38

On necks,

in pages.

Growing necks
                                  bellies
in those I know

books,
kaleidoscopes

genitals

gathered

between glass

39

Al sitio

de antes

39

To the place

from before

40

Se dificulta el pasaje

de relieve a
luz

            a tiempo

a frente
a cerbatana

se dificulta   el rostro

Se ausenta el
punto

larga proliferación donde la hermosura es
lo que no
ve

40

The voyage grows difficult

highlighted by
light

              by time

by brow
by blowgun

the face   grows difficult.

The period goes
missing

long proliferation where beauty is
what is not
seen

41

Caminar con   todo.

Labio

Línea

Hueco.

Alrededor   aire
libros,

otro. Tildar al viento de alguien, encaminar

gestos.

(Llegar hacia
atrás.   Reproducir

día
lazo

cuerpo)

41

To walk with everything.

Lip

Line

Hollow.

Around air
books,

another. Name the wind after someone, direct

gestures toward.

(Arrive
behind.   Reproduce

day
ribbon

body)

42

La gente se extraña

y el tiempo es esa
torva, dos espacios una y otra

vez.

(No hay un espacio uno
　desdoblado

　　cosa　　　en　　imagen
　　　　　　　en　　voz
　　　　　　　en　　sitio

　dura, como cuerpo que sabe.

　Quedar　　　　se

　Fecha sin objeto

　luz)

42

People are estranged

and time is that
severity, two spaces once and once

again.

(There is no single space one
   unfolded

   thing   in   image
              in   voice
              in   place

   hard, like a body that knows.

   Re   main

   Objectless date

   light)

43

Renunciar a   muerte

Asesinar los símbolos donde hay   sangres
que transformar
en sangre.

Señor   la muerte
                    la

perennidad.
Orgías
que no tienen
                    ruido

43

Renounce   death.

Murder symbols where are   bloods
which become
blood.

Lord   death
                    con

tinuity.
Orgies
that make no
              sound

44

Saber   entonces

Quizá porque dos espacios
es
mucho

y dos tiempos   ya

(tal vez,
   si un tiempo solo   ya es
   memoria)

44

To know   then

Perhaps because two spaces
is
many

and two times   now

(perhaps,
   if a single time   is already
   memory)

45

La soledad es:

ínclita.

Descendiente de
nombre
de acto

donde hay   sólo
que hacer   hoy

acto,
nombre.

Leve   allí:

el aire
la cosa   que
se endurece
en aire

45

Solitude is:

illustrious.

Descended from
name
of act

where there is   only
what to do   today

act,
name.

Delicate   there:

air
thing   which
hardens
in air

46

Recorrer el tiempo

su trayectoria   en la caída inhóspita arbitraria
del objeto.

Quedarse allí
sin miedo.   Sin amor.

Escribir: el tiempo objeto en el espacio
                                         sin culpa

sin línea
sin poema.   Al lado del prodigio entonces no será nada

el alma

el libro

el día

ni el prodigio

46

Time runs

   its trajectory   in the inhospitable arbitrary fall
   of the object.

Stay there
without fear.   Without love

Write: time an object in space
                            with no guilt

with no line
with no poem.   At wonder's side there will then be nothing

soul

book

day

no wonder

47

Pesa
el labio.   Y
hay que hacerse de un nombre.   Nada

dice.   El conato de gesto   sólo   ya es

tráfico.   Peso.

Aire.

Aire

47

The lip
weighs.   And
one must make oneself from a name.   Says

nothing   The attempt at gesture   is now   just

traffic.   Weight.

Air.

Air

48

Si tuviese conciencia

digo.   Vano

La necesidad

de tener que revelar   en acto   la finalidad

el gesto

cual revuelta.

Cuando no hay revuelta   en
espectro   solar

48

If there were conscience

I say.   Vanity

The necessity

of having to reveal   in the act   the finality

the gesture

like revolt.

When there is no revolt   in
solar   spectrum

49

Yo   u   otro.

U

como el verbo,
en el acto.

          Aladas:
aquellas cosas que se dan   juntas

línea

curva

49

I   or   another

Or

as the word,
in the act.

         Winged:
those things that are commonly   together

line

curve

50

Y el verbo está en el
acto

amar,
y es tal vez lo contrario

perfecto   en la medida en que
se mira   justo
en su vacío

50

And the word is in the
act

love,
and is perhaps the perfect

opposite   in the measurement where
it sees itself   precisely
in its emptiness

51

Se abre   el ojo

solo.

Se orienta.

Cuando los nudillos lo cierran
                              creyendo,

el ojo se abre

fauce.

Es el
vano.

Y el ojo lee   poema

fauce

51

The single眼eye

opens.

Orients itself.

When knuckles close it
                        believing,

the eye opens

jaw.

It is
vanity.

And the eye reads   poem

jaw

52

Hay que decir   algo

Huir de la palabra del otro.

Sin reír.   La capacidad

del verbo
como aguja.   Un equilibrio.

La ordenación del aire

52

Must say   something

Flee from the other's word

Without laughing.   The word's

capacity
as water.   A balance.

The ordering of air

53

Hablar para que la sangre
diga algo

Cualquier sangre.   El deseo
no es libro
no es palabra.

La cosa es,

y humo,
estatua

53

Speak so that blood
says something

Any blood.   Desire
is no book
is no word.

The thing is,

and smoke,
statue

54

Poemario, se ha dicho.

El deseo no es libro
no es palabra   el libro cierra
la boca
los labios,   abre
el puño

la satisfacción cierra
la boca
los labios

el libro no es carne
el deseo no es libro
el verbo no es palabra

54

Poems, it was said.

Desire is no book
is no word   the book closes
mouth
lips,   fist
opens

satisfaction closes
mouth
lips

book is no flesh
desire is no book
word is no word

55

Poderío
en el inexistir

solo.

Se desplazan   allí:

la luz

los intervalos.

Ebrio, se está siempre   en el mismo sitio;

Lúcido, en cambio:

en la soledad
en el desorden
en el aura

55

Power
in unexistence

only.

They move   there:

light

intervals.

Drunk, always   in the same place;

Lucid, on the other hand:

in solitude
in disorder
in aura

56

No hay nada más allá
del signo, el aura es

opaca.

Su signo.   sobre todas las
cosas.   Su aura.

La luz se signa.
se tuerce.
Se adquiere.

En los intervalos del aura   el poema

       queda

lava

56

There is nothing beyond
the sign, the aura is

opaque.

Sign.   above all
things.   Aura.

Light signs.
Twists.
Acquires.

In the aura's intervals   the poem

        remains

lava

57

Poderío   unánime
en el inexistir

                    siempre.

Rememorar adelante la misma pasión   lo acabado
 inerte,

el círculo.

O poner atrás un ancla.

Primera vez que hay que escoger
entre la historia   el hombre

la palabra   y el espacio

y la muerte

57

Unanimous   power
in unexistence

           always.

Later remember the same passion   finished   inert,

the circle.

Or place an anchor behind.

The first time one must choose
between history   man

word   and space

and death

58

"Hace falta una distancia

la ceguera

el fuego".

No el labio
No el libro.

No la forma.

Permitirse desear estar   solo.

Liberar el pensamiento   —la soledad siendo

Señor   ese anonadamiento
del permiso
del fuego

del deseo

58

"Blindness

fire

missing distance."

No lip
No book.

No form.

Permit self to desire to be   alone.

Liberate thought   —solitude being

Lord   that confusion
of permission
of fire

of desire

59

Recorrer el tiempo.

Su trayectoria. En la caída inhóspita y arbitraria del objeto.

Quedarse allí sin deber.

En la totalidad
 no en el absoluto.

Sin nada

59

Traverse time.

Its trajectory. In the inhospitable, arbitrary fall of the object.

Remain there without   must.

In the totality
         not in the absolute.

Without nothing

60

Primera   vez.

Primera vez el
gesto.   La
renuncia   El mundo.

Primera vez   el trazo
y ya hacen falta distancias.

La distancia.
El hambre.   La

lucidez.   poderío   ralo
en el existir siempre que el trazo
quede en la línea,

en el párpado
en el aire.

Y así uno aparece   se   es.

Se escucha

se hace

amo

uno.

60

First   time.

First time the
gesture.   The
renunciation.   The world.

First time   the tracing
and now missing distances.

Distance.
Hunger.   Lu

cidity.   power   sparse
in existence may tracing always
remain inside the line,

in eyelid
in air.

And thus one appears   one   is.

Listens

makes

one

master.

61

Dividir la ventana es ver la misma niebla

el peso es el mismo, la interrogación
paralela, localiza, no divide,
recorre por el contrario la frente del que mira mi

frente.

Paralelismo.

Camino.

En mi sitio no se mueve
                      nadie.

Ninguna vez la sangre

siempre el hombre.   Ninguna vez la sangre,

la medida.   El
sueño.   El
arca.   El
otro.   El hombre.

Siempre

uno en esos   sitios

61

To divide the window is to see the same fog

the weight is the same, the parallel
interrogation, localizes, not divides,
on the contrary traverses the brow of he who looks at my

brow.

Parallelism.

Road.

In my place no one
                      moves.

Never once blood

always man.   Never once blood,

the measure.
Sleep.   A
strongbox.   The
other.   Man.

Always

one in those   places

62

Por qué,
si no hay   sino

algo:

trazos.

Borrar esa medida interior
buscar esa medida en que el trazo se obstruya
entre luces
y en páramos,
entre páginas, para que el ojo sepa que el trazo resbala
entre pergaminos   entre

líneas

62

Why,
if there isn't   but

something:

tracings.

Erase that inner measure

seek that measure where tracing obstructs itself
between lights
and in deserts,
between pages, that the eye may know tracing slips
between scrolls   between

lines

63

Jamás el relámpago ha reflejado a la luz

la irrealidad
al
 cauce.

Señor.

Jamás la ficción
a la   fuente
el intervalo a su
           nombre

63

Never has lightning reflected
light

unreality
to
　　　riverbed.

Lord.

Never has fiction reflected
the　　source
the interval its
　　　　　name

64

Jamás la muerte
a la inmovilidad

de un verbo
de una efigie

Jamás la muerte
a la inmovilidad
                viva

jamás la espesura
a la muerte

la muerte
a lo otro:

la muerte
el hecho

64

Never death
to the stillness

of a word
of an effigy

Never death
to living
        stillness

never density
to death

death
to the other:

death
fact

65

Jamás el   hombre.

Sólo

uno

65

Never   man

Only

one

66

Ninguna vez　　acá

el sonido
el flujo,

la intensidad.　　Sólo　　el
fluido. El ruido.

Grafismo

　　　　　　　pienso
del aire

en uno

66

Never   once   here

sound
flow,

intensity.   Only   the
fluid. The noise

Graphics

          I think
of air

in one

67

Sin unidad.

Sin rastro: toda esa antigüedad del aire

ubicua

        como la cerbatana

en la imagen   de un ojo
                           sin ubicuidad
                           sin lecho
                           sin medida

dónde.

67

Without unity.

Without a trace: all that antiquity of air

ubiquitous

        as a blowgun

in the image   of an eye

                      with no ubiquity
                      with no bed
                      with no measure

where.

68

En la réplica.

En el labio.

Súplica   en un reflejo.

Así es
              deseo de peso
en la efigie
                    sólo

deseo de muerte en la

palabra

68

In the answer.

On the lip.

Plea   in a reflection.

Thus is
         desire for weight
in the effigy
            alone

desire for death in the

word

69

No se
     el de hoy
infinitivo.

Virgen.

La palabra   sola
llena

sólo colma   transfigura
                                       sin cambio.

El cuerpo solo ya con frecuencia   hace fuego
                                                palabra
                                                crea el vacío
en el labio

              loa,

revierte al labio

sin aura
sin aire
sin poema

69

Not to be
        today's
infinitive.

Virgin

The word   alone
full

alone fulfills   transfigures
                             unchanging.

The body alone now frequently   makes fire
                                           word
                                           creates void
on the lip

        praises,

reverts to lip

with no aura
with no air
with no poem

70

Uno   soy

el que habla   el que signa.

La cosa
intercambiable.   El deseo
se muda   de raya a

humo.   Otras palabras.

Señor   cuando se piensa

la muerte   la nota

el palio

70

One   I am

who speaks   who signs.

Interchangeable
thing.   Desire
muted   from line to

smoke.   Other words.

Lord   when thought

death   note

canopy

71

El intervalo   del hombre.

Por qué,

si no hay derredor   de la palabra.

Si el deseo no restaura   no es epicentro   así

como la muerte   no se agranda
                     no es medida   (y el ruido

no es medida, y el agua

no es medida,

no es miembro

71

The interval   of man.

Why,

if word has no   circumference.

If desire doesn't restore   isn't epicenter   thus

as death   does not increase
              is not measure   (and noise

is not measure, and water

is not measure,

is not member

72

Percepción arrinconada en la vista

(y luego: el saber. Cataclismos del
ojo, su posibilidad sola ya arrecia el miembro
 precipita el miembro

Inaugura, tal vez. Vierte
en el que está de pie:

reliquias

intervalos)

72

Perception cornered in the gaze

(and then: knowing.   Cataclysms of the
eye, its possibility   alone   now   intensifies the part
                                                    precipitates the part

Inaugurates, perhaps.   Pours
on the bystander:

relics

intervals)

73

Luego: el saber

sin reclamos.   A todo lo largo   no augura
no hace mella, la palabra cumple
sobre el vientre, lo cubre   lo procrea   lo aclimata

no hace mella.   No

renuncia.

Su simple posibilidad   vacía
                                          atemoriza
                                          dura

me instaura   ya

declive
falla

canto

73

Then: knowing

without lures.   Along its whole length   does not augur
makes no impression, word carried out
over belly, covers it   procreates   acclimates

makes no impression.   Does not

renounce.

Its simple possibility   empty
                           frightens
                           endures

now   establishes me

decline
fall

song

74

Esperar. Sentir caer

el cobertor   el lienzo.   Obviar esa capacidad sin contorno

    eminentemente afuera de acaparar en el lecho   creencias
                                                                             substancia

                                                                               creación

en el cuerpo.   Y manifestar silencio

en el acto,
en las manos.

Vertiente.   Declive

falla

borde   impalpable

donde el lienzo

cae

74

To wait.   To feel fall

blanket   canvas.   Avoid that contourless capacity

eminently outside of underbed hoarding of   beliefs
                                                                                                      substances

                                                                                                      creation

on the body.   And manifest silence

in the act,
in the hands.

Slope.   Decline

fall

impalpable   edge

where the canvas

falls

75

No saber

Esperar   por ejemplo
el seno.

Retener: la poquedad   infinita
del soplo
de un labio   o

aquella religión   lenta   en sola resistencia
física:

en dos pesos

(Ver.

         cómo la tierra es el gesto

75

To not know

To wait   for example

breast

Retain: the smallness   infinite

of breath
of a lip   or

that slow   religion   in the only physical

resistance:

in two weights,

(See.

        how earth is the gesture

76

Cual inmigrancias:

el deseo no pasa en efecto de una axila   a otra

se vierte: una palabra por   otra

en el intervalo
en el palio, en la
definición.   Jamás el cuerpo

                              sin órgano
                              sin lecho

                              sin palabra

donde el rayo   solo

es evidente

76

Like immigrations:

desire effectively doesn't pass from one shoulder   to the other

it pours: one word through   another

in the interval
in the canopy, in the
definition.   Never the body

                                    without organs
                                    without bed

                                    without word

where only   lightning

is evident

77

Donde todo se dice
y nada sucederá
en el centro,

en una y otra sien, en uno y otro labio
                                                   cuerpo

para los hurtos del   día

El cuerpo allí
se lee   se ora

no es

77

Where everything's said
and nothing will happen
in the center,

on one and the other temple, one and the other lip
                                                                                 body

for the day's   thefts

There the body
reads   prays

is not

78

Mirar,

sin que el ojo se distraiga

No mirar   Sólo allá el centro será

palia

sitio sin nombre   habla,

para que el cuerpo quede

sin sobresalto
sin aura

78

To look,

without distracted eye

To not look   Only there the center will be

a pall

nameless place   speech,

so the body   remains

without distress
without aura

79

Reflujos

Qué cosa es espontánea.   Caminando
el pasado está   adelante

un tiempo sólo   ya es memoria
dos espacios un gesto

                                         el ojo
                                         el libro

lo espontáneo no surge en la
mira   en la sangre.   Muere

de efigies

79

Ebbs

What is spontaneous.   Walking
the past is   ahead

a single time   is now memory
two spaces one gesture

                        the eye
                        the book

the spontaneous does not arise in the
gaze   in the blood.   It dies

of effigies

80

Reverberación de tiempo.

Recorrido

instantáneo

Lo espontáneo no surge en la bala

Demasiado cuerpo en la aparición
del lugar
demasiado lugar tal vez para el área
de un cuerpo

Recóndito
simple

(La sensación bifurca y troca.

No convierte)

80

Reverberation   of time.

Instantaneous

traversal

The spontaneous does not arise in the bullet

Too much body in the apparition
of place
too much place perhaps   for the area
of a body

Hidden
simple

(The sensation forks   turns into.

Does not become.)

81

El sitio.

El hecho.

Precipitación   sin milicias   el cuerpo
no sabe el flujo del   área   en la superficie

el área   no tiene

piso

Sangre

Señor

para el revés de balas

81

Place.

The fact.

Precipitation   without militias   the body
knows not the flow   of the area   on surface

the area   has no

floor

Blood

Lord

for the backward of bullets

82

Si afirmo: sobrevivir, en los
ángulos

Si afirmo   el centro,
                    ese área   allá
donde en mi sitio   no hay
imagen   —

El ojo bebe el ojo del otro
del sol,
el ojo lee: líneas
borde be bala
sueño

82

If I declare: to survive, in the

angles

If I declare   the center,

                      that area   there

where in my place   there is no

image   —

The eye drinks another's eye

sun's eye,

the eye reads: lines

bullet's edge

sleep

83

Cotidiano del otro

en suma.

Hablar   para que el hombre   la sangre

se anuncien

diario,   o rastro

de uno.

La evacuación es larga.

Y la revelación se rompe

sin membranas
sin aire

83

The other's everyday

in short.

To speak   so that man   blood

announce themselves

daily,   or one's

traces.

Evacuation is long.

And revelation breaks

with no membranes
with no air

84

En el centro   de todo

en aquella reverberación del nombre,

la bala
no es precaria.

Una línea.

La lectura insiste
no se niega.

No hay eco.   Sólo el ojo   que

presta.   La boca.   Las manos, ellas, tantean
hacia lo otro infinito,   y el labio acepta

y el ojo continúa la línea

antigüedad

sin huella

84

In the center   of everything

in that reverberation of name,

bullet
is not precarious.

A line.

Reading insists
denies not.

There is no echo.   Only the eye   which

lends.   The mouth.   Hands, those, fumble
toward the infinite other,   the lip accepts

and the eye continues the line

antiquity

without a trace

85

El arquetipo que faltará

caminando:　　el silencio.

flujo.

Una sangre.

(　Amatorio　　regenerar la seda
en la roca　　como gesta del vulgo

a ver　　　　mira

si el ojo que prosigue　　se sienta, se acomoda

se alínea,
lee el poema de líneas　　sucedidas
sin reacción　　como línea

sin canto　)

85

The archetype shall lack

walking: silence.

flow.

A blood

(Amorous   to regenerate silk
on the rock   like a mass feat

to see   look

if the eye continues   feels, gets comfortable

lines up,
reads the poem of successive   lines
with no reaction   as line

with no song   )

86

Allá en la Historia no hay
palabras. Sólo un flujo　　de muerte

instantánea　　　en el acto　　　como en el eructo
no hay puente　　　para el otro

(　El flujo no es novicio. El ojo calla　　　siempre.

El ruido

cesa　)

86

There in History there are no
words. Only a flow   of death

instantaneous   in the act   as a belch
there is no bridge   for the other

(　The flow is no beginner. The eye falls silent   ever.

The noise

halts　)

87

No suprimir   Señor: la línea es fija, no te impide

Repetir: la bala es
perentoria.   y predecir el apogeo siniestro

del ojo

para siempre.

Repetir: la palabra es
lo que queda

Repetir que el lienzo no penetra
que el flujo   no tropieza

87

To not strike down   Lord: the line is fixed, impedes you not

To repeat: the bullet is
urgent.   and to predict the sinister apogee

of the eye

forever.

To repeat: the word is
what remains

To repeat, the canvas does not penetrate
the flow does not   stumble

88

En la Historia.

En el libro.   Un fluido apenas
como signo de flujo   Silencio

como signo de ruido.

(La bala no se aloja en uñas   no atraviesa

viajes

no se aloja   en cataratas

bancos

moratorios   )

su carne   opaca

palia

88

In History.

In the book.   Barely fluid
as a sign of flow   Silence

as a sign of noise.

(The bullet doesn't lodge in fingernails   doesn't cross

travels

doesn't lodge   in cataracts

benches

moratoria   )

your flesh   opaque

pall

89

No hay réplica.   El eco también fluye.

El ojo niega que lee   y
perfecciona la línea, una articulación sin embargo
del labio   le basta para definir
a un prójimo
a un labio.

Naturalismo del aire en el peso
del ojo   lastre

sin aire

memoria con solo   cuerpo

Señor,

con similitud,

sin prójimos

89

There is no reply.   The echo also flows.

The eye denies that it reads   and
perfects line, still an articulation
of the lip   enough to define
a fellow
a lip.

Naturalism of air in the weight
of eye   ballast

without air

memory with only   body

Lord,

with similitude,

without fellows

90

Inventario de estruendos: el
elegir   rampa.

Repertoriar el segmento que corre
en la palabra, la serenidad

que sobra.   Detener
el aire que queda   en las gestas

pocilga   retirada
en milicias, campamentos

suelo fijo

donde no se averiguará trayectos
ni moradas

90

Inventory of thunder: the
choice   incline.

Make a repertory of segment that runs
in the word, serenity

in surplus.   Halt
the air that remains   in feats

pigsty   withdrawal
in militias, encampments

fixed ground

where neither trajectories nor dwellings
are verified

91

Enceguecer miradas.

Ubicar el circuito del
habla.   El deseo se invierte

y es deseo   en la serenidad

del color
de un surco

de la bala

el repertorio

el blanco

La mirada

91

To blind gazes.

To find the circuit of
speech.　　Desire inverted

and is desire　　in serenity

of color
of furrow

of bullet

repertory

target

gaze

92

Señor.

La palabra se extravía en el nombre.

El nombre   roza
perros

harpas

Eunucos se entreveran

no en el fuego,
no en las cimas.

Averiguan decorados:
madrigueras para
bocas
balas

cantos

92

Lord.

The word gets lost in the name.

The name   grazes
dogs

harps

Eunuchs mingle

not with the fire,
nor on the peaks.

They verify scenery:
burrows for
mouths
bullets

songs

93

Vivos.

La luz expulsa caminantes   la permanencia

no tiene filo
como las cabelleras

no hiere,
no protesta

el sitio se encarna,

en intuición

sin bordes

93

The living.

Light expels travelers permanence

has no edge
like hair

does not wound,
does not protest

place incarnates,

in intuition

without edges

94

Múltiplo de luz:

ningún deseo se fija. La bala
se saca de bolsillos
 como intuición,

como nombres.

Lugares.

Ningún letargo falla

sombra,
en la infamia inmaculada

del sol

94

Multiple of light:

no desire is fixed.　　　The bullet
comes out of pockets
　　　　　　　　　　　like intuition,

like names.

Places.

No lethargy fails

shadow,
in the immaculate　　　infamy

of the sun

95

Múltiplo de luz: nada se empaña   en la noche

en el día la sed tampoco sangra   O sólo
se determina,
la sangre, como
en reposo.

No se pregunta.   Y no hay respuesta.
El espacio retenido al término
en un punto   se carga de dorso de lejanías

en el mito
la llaga

no supura

95

Multiple of light: nothing dampens   in the night

neither does thirst bleed during day   Or only
determines itself,
blood, as when
at rest.

Asks no questions.   And there is no answer.
Space retained   to the end
at a point   loads its back with distances

in myth
the sore

does not fester

96

Múltiplo de luz: Señor

el dorso se ve.

La majestad del dolor   la infamia del fuego

es:

adjetivo en el nombre
ruta en la frente:

la cosa se limpia la mirada
para que la sangre
                          sin cosas

sin nadie

no proteste

96

Multiple of light: Lord

the back visible.

The majesty of pain infamy of fire

is:

adjective in name
route on brow:

thing cleans the gaze
so blood

                      with no things

with no one

does not protest

97

El vano se presta al
fondo.
A la mirada sin fondo.   Escarnio

Señor,
para que el ojo se entrevere
en la velocidad de la sangre

para que eunucos

días

                      gestas de eunucos

se crispen   en la perennidad   protectora

del hombre

97

Vanity lends itself to the
bottom.
To bottomless gaze.   Scorn

Lord,
so the eye mingles
in the velocity of blood

so that eunuchs

days

              feats of eunuchs

tense up   in the protective   perenniality

of man

98

El ave es

hombre

fuego.

No soy yo

el fuego:

duración de gesta
en un codo puesto:

demarcación no fugitiva

no siempre

de aire
de respiración

de anatemas

98

The bird is

man

fire.

I am not

fire:

feat's   duration
in an elbow placed:

demarcation   not fugitive

not forever

of air
of respiration

of anathema

99

Vertiente   sólo.

Sólo un ángulo   apenas,
la anfractuosidad
de una línea
en su transcurso.

Y es la medida.   El
protectorado   la rampa

un intersticio.

Información

para una muerte
verosímil

diurna

99

Only   incline.

Only angle   barely,
anfractuosity
of line
in its course.

And is the measure.   The
protected   the incline

a gap.

Information

for a death
diurnal

plausible

100

Finalidad
pasada

sangre

imperfecta

perennidad

aparente
        la del gesto

poema

como un intervalo

de la luz

Bruselas.
Setiembre — Diciembre 1980.
Mayo — Setiembre 1981.

100

Past
finality

imperfect

blood

apparent

perenniality
          of gesture

poem

as interval

of light

      Brussels
      September–December 1980
      May–September 1981

Acknowledgments

Work on this book came at a difficult time, personally and politically, and could not have been completed without the efforts of many. Among them are:

Haley Springer and her daughter Josephine, who kept me grounded and engaged.

Renáto Gómez, who published these poems in Peru, and Mariana Fernández, Gastón's sister, who patiently permitted this project to bear fruit over more than a decade.

Everyone at World Poetry Books, beginning with my editor Matvei Yankelevich, as well as Anne Osherson, Ariel Courage, and especially Roz Shayan Naimi, whose editorial notes on a challenging bilingual manuscript were some of the best I have ever seen.

The editors and staff at *World Poetry Review* and *Asymptote*, where some of these translations appeared.

And the supporters of Celtic Football Club of Glasgow, Scotland, especially The Bhoys and The Green Brigade, whose political clarity and activist example picked me up and pushed me forward again and again, and who never let me forget I do not walk alone.

Gastón Fernández Carrera (1940–1997) was born in Lima, Peru. He studied literature and law in Peru, which he left in the mid-1960s, eventually settling in Belgium, where he earned a degree in art history. As a professional scholar, Fernández worked in French. His literary work in Spanish was all but unknown in his lifetime, with just a few stories appearing in Latin American journals. Posthumous publications of his poems and stories revealed a career of great literary significance.

KM Cascia is the translator of Mexican modernist Manuel Maples Arce's *Stridentist Poems* (World Poetry, 2023). Born in Michigan City, Indiana, Cascia left school at the age of 17 and picked up Spanish working in restaurant kitchens in Chicago, Philadelphia, and New York. Formerly an editor of the translation journals *Calque* and *Asymptote*, they have published four collections of their own poems and their translations of Latin American poetry have appeared in numerous magazines, including *Apiary*, *Circumference*, and *Anomalous*.

This book was typeset in Martina Plantijn, a contemporary serif that celebrates Belgium's rich typographic heritage. Designed by Kris Sowersby in 2023 for the Klim Type Foundry, it draws inspiration from the work of sixteenth-century Antwerp printer Christophe Plantin. His daughter Martina worked in his shop from the age of five and took over the business in 1610. Cover design by Andrew Bourne. Typesetting by Don't Look Now. Printed and bound in Lithuania by BALTO Print. Manufactured by Arctic Paper in Sweden, the paper in this book meets EU Ecolabel, Forest Stewardship Council, and Cradle to Cradle certification standards.

 WORLD POETRY

Marie-Noëlle Agniau
The Escapades
tr. Jesse Hover Amar

Nadia Anjuman
Smoke Drifts: Selected Poems
tr. Diana Arterian & Marina Omar

Jean-Paul Auxeméry
Selected Poems
tr. Nathaniel Tarn

Boethius
The Poems from On the Consolation of Philosophy
tr. Peter Glassgold

Maria Borio
Transparencies
tr. Danielle Pieratti

Astrid Cabral
Spotlight on the Word
tr. Alexis Levitin

Jeannette L. Clariond
Goddesses of Water
tr. Samantha Schnee

Jacques Darras
John Scotus Eriugena at Laon
tr. Richard Sieburth

Mario dell'Arco
Day Lasts Forever: Selected Poems
tr. Marc Alan Di Martino

Marie de Quatrebarbes
The Vitals
tr. Aiden Farrell

Olivia Elias
Chaos, Crossing
tr. Kareem James Abu-Zeid

Gastón Fernández
Apparent Breviary
tr. KM Cascia

Jerzy Ficowski
Everything I Don't Know
tr. Jennifer Grotz & Piotr Sommer
PEN AWARD FOR POETRY IN TRANSLATION

Antonio Gamoneda
Book of the Cold
tr. Katherine M. Hedeen & Víctor Rodríguez Núñez

Mireille Gansel
Soul House
tr. Joan Seliger Sidney

Óscar García Sierra
Houston, I'm the problem
tr. Carmen Yus Quintero

Phoebe Giannisi
Homerica
tr. Brian Sneeden

Zuzanna Ginczanka
On Centaurs & Other Poems
tr. Alex Braslavsky

Julien Gracq
Abounding Freedom
tr. Alice Yang

Leeladhar Jagoori
What of the Earth Was Saved
tr. Matt Reeck

Nakedness Is My End: Poems from the Greek Anthology
tr. Edmund Keeley

Birhan Keskin
Earthly Conditions: Selected Poems
tr. Öykü Tekten

Jazra Khaleed
The Light That Burns Us
ed. Karen Van Dyck

Judith Kiros
O
tr. Kira Josefsson

Dimitra Kotoula
The Slow Horizon That Breathes
tr. Maria Nazos

Maria Laina
Hers
tr. Karen Van Dyck

Maria Laina
Rose Fear
tr. Sarah McCann

Perrin Langda
A Few Microseconds on Earth
tr. Pauline Levy Valensi

Anna Malihon
Girl with a Bullet
tr. Olena Jennings

Afrizal Malna
Document Shredding Museum
tr. Daniel Owen

Joyce Mansour
In the Glittering Maw: Selected Poems
tr. C. Francis Fisher

Manuel Maples Arce
Stridentist Poems
tr. KM Cascia

Ennio Moltedo
Night
tr. Marguerite Feitlowitz

Meret Oppenheim
The Loveliest Vowel Empties: Collected Poems
tr. Kathleen Heil

Giovanni Pascoli
Last Dream
tr. Geoffrey Brock
RAIZISS/DE PALCHI TRANSLATION AWARD

Gabriel Pomerand
Saint Ghetto of the Loans
tr. Michael Kasper & Bhamati Viswanathan

Liliana Ponce
Theory of the Voice and Dream
tr. Michael Martin Shea

Rainer Maria Rilke
Where the Paths Do Not Go
tr. Burton Pike

Amelia Rosselli
Document
tr. Roberta Antognini & Deborah Woodard

Elisabeth Rynell
Night Talks
tr. Rika Lesser

Waly Salomão
Border Fare
tr. Maryam Monalisa Gharavi

George Sarantaris
Abyss and Song: Selected Poems
tr. Pria Louka

George Seferis
Book of Exercises II
tr. Jennifer R. Kellogg

Seo Jung Hak
The Cheapest France in Town
tr. Megan Sungyoon

Ahmad Shamlou
Elegies of the Earth: Selected Poems
tr. Niloufar Talebi

Ardengo Soffici
Simultaneities & Lyric Chemisms
tr. Olivia E. Sears

Liesl Ujvary
Good & Safe
tr. Ann Cotten & Anna-Isabella Dinwoodie

Paul Verlaine
Before Wisdom: The Early Poems
tr. Keith Waldrop & K.A. Hays

Witold Wirpsza
Apotheosis of Music
tr. Frank L. Vigoda

Uljana Wolf
kochanie, today i bought bread
tr. Greg Nissan

Ye Lijun
My Mountain Country
tr. Fiona Sze-Lorrain

Verónica Zondek
Cold Fire
tr. Katherine Silver